GIRLFRIENDS

GIRLFRIENDS

a celebration

Lawrence Teacher Books
=== Philadelphia ===

Copyright ©2005 by Lawrence Teacher Books

Printed in China. All rights reserved.

Mechanicals produced by book soup publishing, inc.

Cover and interior design by Carole Goodman/BLUE ANCHOR
DESIGN

Quotes compiled by Melissa Lieberman
Edited by Erin Slonaker

This book may not be reproduced in any form or by any
means without written permission of the publisher.

ISBN 1-930408-03-X

10 9 8 7 6 5 4 3 2 1

Please support your local book or gift store. However, if you
cannot find this book there, you may order it directly from
the publisher. Please add $1.50 for postage and handling.
Send check or money order to the address below.

LAWRENCE TEACHER BOOKS
1 PEARL BUCK COURT, BRISTOL, PA. 19007

There's a magical bond that unites women in friendship. We may have different goals, different lives, and different opinions, but somewhere deep down we find that the similarities we share are the most important.

It's with our girlfriends that we find solace from the rest of the world. We go to each other for comfort, for support, and even for a laugh. Many of us plan a special "girls' night out" whenever possible.

When we're with our girl-
friends, more than any other
relationship, we find that
it's easiest to be just who
we are and nothing more.

Together we can discuss
anything and everything,
from politics to fashion to
philosophy to relationships.
Our perspective as women

lends a unique insight on any topic we choose. We are always learning from our girlfriends, becoming better people, better women.

This little book is a collection of quotes from women honoring that special bond, those special friends whom we call *girlfriends*.

True friendship
between women
is rare, I know,
but we were
never disloyal.

Anita Brookner
BRITISH WRITER
(B. 1928)

I found real love in girlfriends.

Tina Turner
AMERICAN SINGER
(B. 1938)

I always felt that the great high privilege, relief, and comfort of friendship was that one had to explain nothing.

Katherine Mansfield
BRITISH WRITER
(1888–1923)

We were united
by a common
bond of interest.
We spoke each
other's language.

Ruth Rowland Nichols
AMERICAN AVIATOR
(1901–1961)

Female friendships
are like no other
relationship: uncon-
ditional, loving, silly,
silly, safe. They are
our secret weapon.

Beverly Lowry
20TH CENTURY AMERICAN WRITER

The connections between
and among women are
the most feared, the most
problematic, and the most
potentially transforming
force on the planet.

Adrienne Rich
AMERICAN POET
(B. 1929)

In the world of relationships,
possibly the most complicated,
uncommon, hard to find, hard
to keep, and most rewarding
has got to be friendship.

Lauren Bacall
AMERICAN ACTOR
(B. 1924)

Friendship is about commitment and loyalty. I don't think it matters how far apart you are. I don't see some of my

girlfriends for
ages, but when
we get together
it is as if time
hasn't passed.

Frances Barber
BRITISH ACTRESS
(B. 1958)

The growth of true friend- ship may be a lifelong affair.

Sarah Orne Jewett
AMERICAN WRITER
(1849–1909)

Now I seem to have a pack of real-life female buddies, these smart, intelligent women who are celebrating the power of female friendship— girlfriend power.

Rebecca Wells
20TH CENTURY AMERICAN WRITER

We need old friends
to help us grow old
and new friends to
help us stay young.

Letty Cottin Pogrebin
AMERICAN WRITER
(B. 1939)

The most called-upon prerequisite of a friend is an accessible ear.

Maya Angelou
AMERICAN WRITER
(B. 1928)

If one could be friendly with women, what a pleasure— the relationship so secret and private compared with relations with men.

Virginia Woolf
BRITISH WRITER
(1882–1941)

After an acquaintance of ten minutes many women will exchange confidences that a man would not reveal to a lifelong friend.

Page Smith
AMERICAN HISTORIAN, WRITER
(B. 1917)

Girls and women become more authentic through their friends.

Pat Ross
AMERICAN WRITER
(B. 1943)

It's been wonderful to have a best friend who knew me before this whirl-wind. Somebody I can go home to. Somebody who knows what's real.

Jennifer Aniston
AMERICAN ACTOR
(B. 1969)

... as nobody can do more mischief to a woman than a woman, so perhaps might one reverse the maxim and say nobody can do more good.

Lady Elizabeth Holland
BRITISH SALONIST
(1771–1845)

The bond
between women
is a circle—we
are together
within it.

Judy Grahn
AMERICAN POET, WRITER
(B. 1940)

What would we do without our women friends? I can't imagine how we could survive without the hugs and humor, the closeness and Kleenex that our female friendships provide.

Cookie Roberts
AMERICAN NEWS ANALYST
(B. 1943)

My friends
have made the
story of my life.

Helen Keller
AMERICAN WRITER, EDUCATOR
(1880–1968)

The depth of a friendship—how much it means to us—depends, at least in part, upon how many parts of ourselves a friend sees, shares, and validates.

Lillian Rubin
20TH CENTURY AMERICAN WRITER

Lots of people want to ride with you in the limo, but what you want is someone who will take the bus with you when the limo breaks down.

Oprah Winfrey
AMERICAN ACTOR,
TALK-SHOW HOST
(B. 1954)

Good books, like good friends, are few and chosen; the more select, the more enjoyable.

Louisa May Alcott
AMERICAN WRITER
(1832–1888)

We have a great
respect for each other
and we trust each other.
That's what a great
friendship is, whether
we talk every day or not.

Jennifer Azzi
AMERICAN PRO
BASKETBALL PLAYER
(B. 1969)

True friendship is like phosphorescence—it glows best when the world around you goes dark.

Denise Martin
AMERICAN WRITER
(B. 1940)

We rarely talk of sex the way
men do, in terms of I've had
this one, I've had that one.
There's a friend I've known
for 19 years and all I've
known of her private life is
what I've heard from others.

Jeanne Moreau
FRENCH ACTRESS
(B. 1928)

Understand that friendship arrives from the least likely sources and flourishes in the least likely locations. Understand that someone can know you very well though you have not told her about yourself.

Whitney Otto
AMERICAN WRITER
(B. 1955)

We know that we are all bound by the life stories we divulge to our friends, whether they be about the highs, the lows, or even the in-betweens of life. We nod with sympathetic murmurs and accept the truth because we truly love each other, we women do.

Lois Wyse
AMERICAN WRITER,
ADVERTISING EXECUTIVE
(B. 1926)

Each friend represents
a world in us, a world
possibly not born until
they arrive, and it is only
by this meeting that a
new world is born.

Anaïs Nin
FRENCH-AMERICAN WRITER
(1903–1977)

It is curious that it may be the help of a housekeeper and a friend that facilitates a woman's life work, while the closest analogy . . . one would find from the pen of a man is typically a tribute to his wife.

Alice Rossi
AMERICAN EDUCATOR, WRITER
(B. 1922)

It is a rare and special thing to find a friend who will remain a friend forever.

Ruth Langdon Morgan
AMERICAN WRITER
(1878–1940)

As time went on, we grew stronger together and became like sisters. It was nice having somebody around that I could trust and tell anything to, knowing it would stay with her until she leaves this planet.

Patti LaBelle
AMERICAN SINGER
(B. 1944)

It seemed to me that those women were conducting the most important business in the world as they talked together and that they were having a whole lot of fun doing it. The warm, reciprocal, nurturing friendship they shared was one of the reasons I wanted to grow up to be a woman.

Susan Koppelman
20TH CENTURY AMERICAN WRITER, EDITOR, EDUCATOR

Often intimacies
between women
go backwards, begin-
ning with revelations
and ending up in
small-talk without
loss of esteem.

Elizabeth Bowen
BRITISH WRITER
(1899–1973)

Girls' emotional lives are lived with their girlfriends.

Terri Apter
    20TH CENTURY BRITISH WRITER,
    PSYCHOLOGIST,

& Ruthellen Josselson
    20TH CENTURY AMERICAN WRITER,
    PSYCHOTHERAPIST

It's mutual support once the competition is ruled out. With women friendships, you're comrades in the battle of life.

Miriam Lacob
20TH CENTURY SOUTH AFRICAN WRITER

Her deepest
heart's desire
cannot be satisfied
by the circum-
stances of her
birth, by material
finery, by a father,

a mother, or a brother, but only by a friendship of her choosing with another girl.

Amy Ling
20TH CENTURY AMERICAN WRITER, PROFESSOR

Friendships aren't perfect and yet they are precious.

Letty Cottin Pogrebin
AMERICAN WRITER
(B. 1939)

After the age of forty there isn't much to live for except friendship.

Francine du Plessix Gray
POLISH-AMERICAN WRITER
(B. 1930)

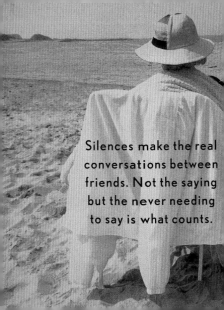

Silences make the real conversations between friends. Not the saying but the never needing to say is what counts.

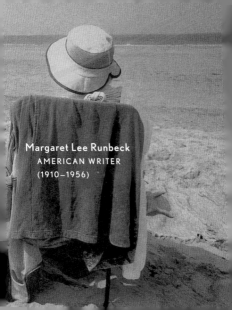

Margaret Lee Runbeck
AMERICAN WRITER
(1910–1956)

True friends are those who really know you but love you anyway.

Edna Buchanan
AMERICAN JOURNALIST
(B. 1946)

The loneliest woman in
the world is a woman without
a close woman friend.

Toni Morrison
AMERICAN WRITER
(B. 1931)

Friendship's a noble name, 'tis love refined.

Susannah Centlivre
BRITISH PLAYWRIGHT
(1669–1723)

Even in old age, these
two women nurtured their
friendship. They kept a
steady stream of notes and
gifts flowing between them,
relishing the comfort and joy
of a lifelong friendship.

Margaret Truman
AMERICAN FIRST DAUGHTER
(B. 1924)

You can date the evolving life of a mind, like the age of a tree, by the rings of friendship formed by the expanding central trunk.

Mary McCarthy
AMERICAN WRITER
(1912–1989)

Great friendships with women are some of life's most difficult and caring intimacies. If I work harder at them, I hope to have them forever.

Wendy Wasserstein
AMERICAN PLAYWRIGHT
(B. 1950)

You don't know
a woman until
you have had a
letter from her.

Ada Leverson
BRITISH WRITER
(1862–1933)

When the sun shines
on you, you see your
friends. Friends are
the thermometers
by which one may
judge the temperature
of our fortunes.

Lady Marguerite Blessington
IRISH WRITER
(1789–1849)

Female friendships
that work are rela-
tionships in which
women help each
other belong to
themselves.

Louise Bernikow
AMERICAN WRITER
(B. 1940)

I don't think any woman
in power really has a happy life
unless she's got a large number
of women friends—because you
sometimes must go and sit down
and let down your hair with
someone you can trust totally.

Margaret Thatcher
BRITISH PRIME MINISTER
(B. 1925)

Few comforts are more alluring for a woman than the rich intimate territory of women's talk. A woman friend will say, "You are not alone. I have felt that way, too. This is what happened to me." Home, in other words.

Elsa Walsh
AMERICAN JOURNALIST, WRITER
(B. 1959)

There were equal
measures of comfort
and amusement in our
communications; I think
it is safe to say that we
delighted in one another.

Jane Hamilton
AMERICAN WRITER
(B. 1957)

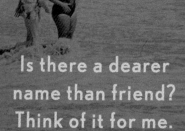

Is there a dearer
name than friend?
Think of it for me.

Abigail Adams

AMERICAN FIRST LADY

(1744–1818)

When I was younger, I had more male friends than female friends. Now I've come to realize how rewarding women friends can be. There can be real love between girlfriends.

Donna Mills
AMERICAN ACTOR
(B. 1943)

Only by becoming friends with other women, by understanding what we share and don't share, can we truly begin to know what it is to be a woman today.

Judith Finlayson
20TH CENTURY AMERICAN WRITER

Girls especially are fond of exchanging confidences with those who they think they can trust; it is one of the most charming traits of a simple, earnest-

hearted girlhood,
and they are
the happiest
women who never
lose it entirely.

Lucy Larcom
AMERICAN POET, MILL WORKER
(1824–1893)

My girlfriends are the sisters I picked out for myself.

Mary-Margaret Martinez
AMERICAN WRITER
(B. 1960)

Friends, no matter how far separated, will grow in love and sympathy and nearness to each other.

Bertha Conde
EARLY 20TH CENTURY
AMERICAN WRITER

I am treating you as my friend, asking you to share my present minuses in the hope I can ask you to share my future pluses.

Katherine Mansfield
BRITISH WRITER
(1888-1923)

Femininity means different things to different women, but being able to celebrate your own womanhood helps you celebrate your women friends.

Carmen Renee Berry & Tamara Traeder
20TH CENTURY AMERICAN WRITERS

The pieces I am,
she gather them
and give them
back to me in all
the right order.

from *Beloved* by
Toni Morrison
AMERICAN WRITER
(B. 1931)

We've been friends longer than we've been people; she's the sister I never had.

Suzanne Finnamore
20TH CENTURY AMERICAN WRITER

We shelter our children for
a time; we live side by side
with men; and that is all. We
owe them nothing, and are
owed nothing. I think we owe
our friends more, especially
our female friends.

Fay Weldon
BRITISH WRITER
(B. 1933)

The friends one's mother chooses for herself lets her daughter see what grown-up female life is like.

Christine O'Hagan
20TH CENTURY AMERICAN WRITER

Through becoming
her friend I became a
better person, and she
said the same of me.

Amanda Cross
AMERICAN WRITER
(B. 1926)

I think women
know how to
be friends.
That's what
saves our lives.

Alice Adams
AMERICAN WRITER
(B. 1926)

Friendship between women can take different forms. It can run like a river, quietly and sustainingly through life; it can be an intermittent, sometime thing; or it can explode like a meteor, altering the atmosphere so that nothing ever feels or looks the same again.

Molly Haskell
AMERICAN CRITIC
(B. 1939)

And we find at the end of a perfect day, the soul of a friend we've made.

Carrie Jacobs Bond
AMERICAN COMPOSER
(1862–1946)

She became for me an island of light, fun wisdom where I could run with my discoveries and torments and hopes at any time of day and find welcome.

May Sarton
AMERICAN POET, WRITER
(1912–1995)

One is taught by experience to put a premium on those few people who can appreciate you for what you are.

Gail Godwin
AMERICAN WRITER
(B. 1937)

Our female friends are forever.

Anna Quindlen
AMERICAN WRITER, COLUMNIST
(B. 1953)

She always knows exactly what I need to boost my spirits and is forever doing the things that bring huge smiles to my face.

Aimee Olivo
AMERICAN WRITER
(B. 1941)

Men kick friendship around like a football, but it doesn't seem to crack. Women treat it like glass and it goes to pieces.

Anne Morrow Lindbergh
AMERICAN WRITER
(B. 1906)

But every road
is tough for me /
That has no friend
to cheer it.

Elizabeth Shane
EARLY 20TH CENTURY IRISH POET

Everyone has a gift
for something, even
if it is the gift of
being a good friend.

Marian Anderson
AMERICAN SINGER
(1902–1993)

The friend who holds
your hand and says the
wrong thing is made of
dearer stuff than the
one who stays away.

Barbara Kingsolver
AMERICAN WRITER
(B. 1955)

The most beautiful discovery true friends make is that they can grow separately without growing apart.

Elisabeth Foley
20TH CENTURY AMERICAN WRITER

Many women understand.
We may share experi-
ences, make jokes, paint
pictures, and describe
humiliations that
mean little to men, but
women understand.

Gloria Steinem
AMERICAN ACTIVIST, EDITOR, WRITER
(B. 1934)

She made me believe in myself. She was hysterically loud and loved noise and a good time. She made me feel okay to be who I was.

Bette Midler
AMERICAN ACTRESS, SINGER
(B. 1945)

Most women would agree. Our friends are among life's greatest treasures. They help us negotiate the difficult hurdles of life.

Brenda Hunter
20TH CENTURY AMERICAN WRITER

In meeting again after a separation, acquaintances ask after our outward life, friends after our inner life.

Marie von
Ebner-Eschenbach
AUSTRIAN WRITER
(1830–1916)

Women's friend-
ships often have
the intensity
of romantic
attachment.

Lucy O'Brien
20TH CENTURY BRITISH WRITER

I suppose there is one friend in the life of each of us who seems not a separate person, however dear and beloved,

but an expansion,
an interpretation,
of one's self, the
very meaning of
one's soul.

Edith Wharton
AMERICAN WRITER
(1862–1937)

Photo Credits